LISTS TO *~~ ~~* BY
—— *for* ——
EVERY MARRIED COUPLE

COMPILED BY ALICE GRAY,
STEVE STEPHENS, JOHN VAN DIEST

Multnomah® Publishers *Sisters, Oregon*

LISTS TO LIVE BY FOR EVERY MARRIED COUPLE
published by Multnomah Publishers, Inc.
" 2001 by Alice Gray, Steve Stephens, and John Van Diest
International Standard Book Number: 1-57673-998-8

Cover and interior designed by Uttley DouPonce DesignWorks, Sisters, Oregon
Cover image by Eyewire

Scripture quotations are from *The Holy Bible,* New International Version
" 1973, 1984 by International Bible Society,
used by permission of Zondervan Publishing House

The lists in this book are not substitutes for obtaining professional advice
from qualified persons and organizations. Consult the appropriate professional
advisor for complete and updated information.

Multnomah is a trademark of Multnomah Publishers, Inc.,
and is registered in the U.S. Patent and Trademark Office.
The colophon is a trademark of Multnomah Publishers, Inc.
Printed in the United States of America
ALL RIGHTS RESERVED

No part of this publication may be reproduced, stored in a retrieval system, or transmitted,
in any form or by any means—electronic, mechanical, photocopying, recording,
or otherwise—without prior written permission.

For information:
MULTNOMAH PUBLISHERS, INC., POST OFFICE BOX 1720
SISTERS, OREGON 97759

Library of Congress Cataloging-in-Publication Data

Lists to live by for every married couple / compiled by Alice Gray,
Steve Stephens, John Van Diest.
    p. cm.
    Includes bibliographical references.
    ISBN 1-57673-998-8 (pbk.)
      1. Marriage. 2. Marriage--Religious aspects--Christianity. I. Gray, Alice, 1939--
II. Stephens, Steve. III. Van Diest, John.
HQ734.L5785 2001
306.81--dc21

                  2001000990

01 02 03 04 05 06 07 08 — 10 9 8 7 6 5 4 3 2 1 0

LISTS TO LIVE BY

for

EVERY MARRIED COUPLE

Other books in the Lists to Live By series:

Lists to Live By: The First Collection

Lists to Live By: The Second Collection

Lists to Live By for Every Caring Family

Lists to Live By for Every Married Couple

Lists to Live By: The Third Collection (December 2001)

Contents

Introduction 9

The Five Love Languages *10*

Things to Say to Your Spouse *12*

Things Not *to Say to Your Spouse* *14*

18 Qualities to Develop in Your Marriage *16*

The Top Ten Mistakes Couples Make *18*

Marital Dating *20*

Fun Activities for Couple Friends *22*

Communicate *24*

Bonds of Intimacy *26*

What Is Love? *29*

What Draws Us Closer to God? *30*

12 Times to Say "I'm Sorry" *32*

Do's *of a Marriage* *34*

Dont's *of a Marriage* *35*

Loving Little Things for Wives to Do *36*

Loving Little Things for Husbands to Do *40*

Five Principles for Authentic Communication *45*

What Prevents Us from Communicating More? *46*

12 Actions for a Successful Marriage *47*

Reigniting the Romance after Age 50 . . . . *48*

How to Make Your Bedroom More Romantic *50*

Nine Ways to E-N-C-O-U-R-A-G-E Each Other *52*

50 Habits for Marriage *54*

Why Is a Healthy Marriage So Important? *59*

True Love... . . . . *60*

Strategies for the Second Half of Marriage *62*

How Well Do We Communicate? *64*

How to Mismanage Conflict *66*

How to Manage Conflict *67*

Seven Resolutions for Your Marriage *69*

20 Ways to Make Your Wife Feel Special *70*

20 Ways to Make Your Husband Feel Special *72*

Between a Husband and Wife *77*

A Regret-Free Marriage *78*

What Makes Marriage Worthwhile? *80*

Ten Suggestions for Touching *82*

What Would Improve Your Sexual Relations? *86*

Tips for the Romantically Challenged *89*

50 Fun Things to Do with Your Spouse *90*

Your Best Friend *94*

How to Be Happy in Marriage *96*

Doing It Together *98*

Trust Builders *100*

Trust Busters *101*

13 Rules for Fighting Fair *102*

Pray for His... . . . . *104*

Pray for Her... . . . . *105*

Pray Together for Our... . . . . *106*

Seven Commitments for a Strong Marriage *109*

What Are Your Dreams? *110*

20 Creative, Romantic Ideas That Cost under $20 . . . . *112*

The 20 Most Romantic Gifts *116*

True Love Is... . . . . *120*

Are You a Great Marrriage Partner? *122*

Four Promises of Forgiveness *124*

Six Steps Toward Reconciliation *125*

21 Things Every Couple Should Know *126*

Talk About How You Want to Celebrate These Holidays *128*

Talk About Your Expectations in These Areas *130*

How to Make Your Marriage Healthy *132*

His Needs, Her Needs *134*

20 Most Romantic Literary Works *136*

20 Most Romantic Songs *138*

Ten Greatest Romance Movies *140*

How to Love Him Unconditionally *142*

How to Love Her Unconditionally *143*

Daily Tips for Your Marriage *144*

When the Situation Is Difficult, Ask... . . . .*147*

Suggestions on How to Serve Your Spouse *148*

Love... . . . .*150*

Ten Reasons Divorce Isn't the Answer *152*

20 Marriage Memories *154*

Talk About These Things *158*

Springboards to Deeper Conversation *160*

How to Be an Affectionate Husband *162*

How to Find the Perfect Gift *164*

Wedding Anniversary Gifts *166*

Faith Affirmations for a Husband *168*

Faith Affirmations for a Wife *169*

Heart-to-Heart *171*

Traditional Marriage Vows *172*

Lists for Our Marriage *173*

Acknowledgments *182*

Introduction

Marriage is wonderful! It isn't always easy, but it's still wonderful.

Whatever shape your marriage is in today, it can be enriched by the quick-to-read and easy-to-apply ideas packed in this treasured resource.

Tender and strong…

Inspiring and practical…

Entertaining and life-changing…

Read the truth and wisdom captured on every page, and discover how you can experience the incredible joy of a marriage that lasts a lifetime.

ALICE GRAY, DR. STEVE STEPHENS, AND JOHN VAN DIEST

The Five Love Languages

1. WORDS OF AFFIRMATION

   Compliments, words of encouragement, and requests rather than demands affirm the self-worth of your spouse.

2. QUALITY TIME

   Spending quality time together through sharing, listening, and participating in joint meaningful activities communicates that we truly care for and enjoy each other.

3. RECEIVING GIFTS

   Gifts are tangible symbols of love, whether they are items you purchased or made or are merely your own presence made available to your spouse. Gifts demonstrate that you care, and they represent the value of the relationship.

4. ACTS OF SERVICE

Criticism of your spouse's failure to do things for you may be
an indication that "acts of service" is your primary love language.
Acts of service should never be coerced but should be freely
given and received, and completed as requested.

5. PHYSICAL TOUCH

Physical touch, as a gesture of love, reaches to the depths of
our being. As a love language, it is a powerful form of communication—from the smallest touch on the shoulder to the
most passionate kiss.

GARY CHAPMAN
From *The Five Love Languages*

Things to Say to Your Spouse

"I love you."

"I was wrong."

"Good job!"

"What would you like?"

"You are wonderful."

"What is on your mind?"

"That was really great."

"Let me just listen."

"I appreciate all the things you've done for me all these years."

"I missed you today."

"You are so special."

"I couldn't get you off my mind today."

"What can I do to help?"

"Pray for me."

"I'm praying for you today."

"I love to see your eyes sparkle when you smile."

"As always, you look good today."

"I trust you."

"Thank you for loving me."

"I can always count on you."

"Thank you for accepting me."

"You make me feel good."

"You make every day brighter."

"I prize every moment we spend together."

"I'm sorry."

DR. STEVE STEPHENS
From *Marriage: Experience the Best*

Things Not *to Say to Your Spouse*

"I told you so."

"I can do whatever I like."

"You're just like your mother."

"If you don't like it, you can just leave."

"You're always in a bad mood."

"Can't you do anything right?"

"You just don't think."

"That was stupid."

"It's your fault."

"All you ever do is think of yourself."

"What's wrong with you?"

"If you really loved me, you'd do this."

"All you ever do is complain."

"You're such a baby."

"I can't do anything to please you."

"Turnabout's fair play."

"You get what you deserve."

"You deserve a dose of your own medicine."

"Why don't you ever listen to me?"

"What's your problem?"

"Can't you be more responsible?"

"I can never understand you."

"What were you thinking?"

"Do you always have to be right?"

"You're impossible!"

"I don't know why I put up with you."

Dr. Steve Stephens
From *Marriage: Experience the Best*

18 Qualities to Develop in Your Marriage

1. Positive attitude

2. Spiritual values

3. Sense of humor

4. Faithfulness

5. Honesty

6. Respect

7. Good communication skills

8. Diligence and hard work

9. Compassion

10. Playfulness

11. Generosity

12. Forgiving spirit

13. Flexibility

14. Confidence

15. Sensitivity

16. Understanding

17. Common sense

18. Wisdom with money

AL AND ALICE GRAY
Married thirty-four years and loving it!

The Top Ten Mistakes Couples Make

1. Avoid conflict. Avoided conflict requires repression of anger, which leads to depression of feelings. A genuinely passionate partnership requires conflict, not terminal niceness or withdrawal.

2. Avoid each other. Occasional withdrawal is healthy. Habitual withdrawal (stonewalling) is death to a partnership.

3. Escalate. Conflict, skillfully handled, is one of the keys to a great relationship. Conflict out of control is an excuse for physical, verbal, or psychological abuse.

4. Criticize. Habitually speaking (or thinking) criticism is hard on a relationship. Criticism is usually a sign that the criticizing partner has some personal development work to do.

5. Show contempt. Contempt is criticism escalated to outright mental abuse.

6. React defensively. Fear is natural. Defensiveness naturally accompanies fear. Skillful partnering requires practicing techniques that allow you to drop the defensiveness despite your fear.

7. Deny responsibility. When you deny your responsibility for your part of the issue, you wind up blaming your partner and trying to change him.

8. Rewrite history. Remembering mainly the negative experiences in a partnership is a predictor of future breakdown. All partnerships have difficult spots.

9. Refuse to get help. Partnership coaching and willingness work!

10. Believe that changing partners is the solution. People may go through several partners while repeatedly avoiding the same issues.

MARTY CROUCH
Partner Coach

Marital Dating

1. Make dating your spouse a top priority.

2. Ask your spouse out formally.

3. Set up regular date nights—block them out on your calendar.

4. Trade off on who plans the dates. (She plans one, then he plans one, then it's her turn again.)

5. Be positive if your partner chooses a place that isn't your favorite. (Remember that it's who you're with, not what you do, that's important.)

6. Be creative and don't get into the rut of doing the same old thing.

7. Make sure you spend some time during the date talking and listening.

8. Don't talk about finances, children, or problems on a date.

9. Be on your very best behavior.

10. Do something romantic.

11. Hold hands.

12. Have fun.

Fun Activities for Couple Friends

Take a trip to the mountains.

Plan a picnic in the park.

Cook dinner together.

Visit a museum.

Go hiking.

Start a book club.

Share prayer requests.

Learn a new card game together.

Rent old movies.

Fly kites.

Attend a play or sporting event.

Explore an arts and crafts fair.

Rest and relax at a recreation area such
as a lake, river, or park.

TRICIA GOYER
Condensed from *HomeLife* magazine

Communicate

Choose to truly listen.

Offer to talk whenever it's important to your spouse.

Meet each other's needs without complaining.

Mind your manners.

Understand that negative words do great damage.

Never go to bed angry.

Initiate physical touching to affirm your love.

Compliment each other daily.

Attend to each other's feelings.

Tell each other about your love.

Express your appreciation to God for bringing the
two of you together.

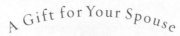

A Gift for Your Spouse

THE GIFT OF SHARING:

Talking about my

hopes and fears and all

that is in my heart.

Bonds of Intimacy

- Physical touching of an affectionate, nonsexual nature

- Shared feelings

- Closeness without inhibitions

- Absence of psychological defenses

- Open communication and honesty

- Intellectual agreement on major issues

- Spiritual harmony

- Sensitive appreciation of your mate's physical and emotional responses

- Similar values held

- Imparted secrets

- Genuine understanding

- Mutual confidence

- A sense of warmth, safety, and realization when together

- Sensuous nearness

- Sexual pleasures lovingly shared

- Signs of love freely given and received

- Mutual responsibility and caring

- Abiding trust

ED WHEAT, M.D.
Condensed from *Love Life for Every Married Couple*

Wisdom *for* Marriage

❧

*To love and be loved is
to feel the sun from both sides.*

BARBARA JOHNSON

*Duty makes us do things well,
but love makes us do them beautifully.*

PHILLIPS BROOKS

*Love is not blind;
love sees a great deal more than the actual.
Love sees the ideas, the potential in us.*

OSWALD CHAMBERS

What Is Love?

1. Love delights in giving attention rather than attracting it.

2. Love finds the element of good and builds on it.

3. Love does not magnify defects.

4. Love is a flame that warms but never burns.

5. Love knows how to disagree without becoming disagreeable.

6. Love rejoices at the success of others instead of being envious.

FATHER JAMES KELLER, founder, "The Christophers"
As cited in *More of...The Best of Bits & Pieces,* Rob Gilbert, Ph.D., editor

What Draws Us Closer to God?

Appreciating nature

Praying

Attending church

Sharing your faith

Helping others

Reading your Bible

Reading devotionals

Showing compassion

Spiritual books

Meditating

Using your gifts

Listening to spiritual music

Going to a Bible study

Speaking to those with similar beliefs

Tithing

Forgiving others

Confessing your sins

Avoiding vices

Memorizing Bibles verses

Doing good

Giving to the poor and needy

DR. STEVE STEPHENS
From *Understanding the One You Love*

12 Times to Say "I'm Sorry"

Say "I'm sorry" (and really mean it) whenever you...

1. Are wrong.

2. Are rude.

3. Are defensive.

4. Are impatient.

5. Are negative.

6. Are hurtful.

7. Are insensitive.

8. Are forgetful.

9. Are confused or confusing.

10. Have neglected, ignored, or overlooked something important to the one you love.

11. Have damaged, misused, or impaired something that is not yours (even if it was an accident).

12. Have not said "I'm sorry" as sincerely and quickly as the situation warranted.

Do's *of a Marriage*

1. Good communication

2. Ability to resolve conflicts

3. Shared interests and goals

4. Flexibility in problem solving

5. Healthy and mutually satisfying sexual relationship

6. Similar spiritual beliefs

7. Financial agreements

8. Fun together

9. Supportive attitude toward each other

10. Mutual respect

Don'ts *of a Marriage*

Don't be angry at each other at the same time.

Don't yell at each other unless the house is on fire.

Don't resist yielding to the wishes of the other.

Don't criticize unlovingly.

Don't bring up mistakes of the past.

Don't let the day end without saying at least one kind or complimentary thing to your spouse.

Don't meet without an affectionate welcome.

Don't let the sun go down on an unresolved argument.

Don't hold pride; ask for forgiveness.

Don't forget: It takes two to make a quarrel, but only one to stop it.

GLENDA HOTTON, M.A.
Counselor

Loving Little Things for Wives to Do

- Pray for your husband daily.

- Show him you love him unconditionally.

- Tell him you think he's the greatest.

- Show him you believe in him.

- Don't talk negatively to him or about him.

- Tell him daily that you love him.

- Give him adoring looks.

- Show him that you enjoy being with him.

- Listen to him when he talks with you.

- Hug him often.

- Kiss him tenderly and romantically.

- Show him that you enjoy the thought of sex.

- Show him you enjoy meeting his sexual needs.

- Take the sexual initiative at times.

- Fix his favorite meal at an unexpected time.

- Demonstrate your dedication to him in public.

- Do things for him he doesn't expect.

- Show others you are proud to be his wife.

- Rub his back, legs, and feet.

- Stress his strengths, not his weaknesses.

- Don't try to mold him into someone else.

- Revel in his joys; share his disappointments.

- Show him your favorite times are with him.

- Show him you respect him more than anyone.

- Don't give him reason to doubt your love.

- Leave "I love you" notes in unexpected places.

- Give him your undivided attention often.

- Tell him he is your "greatest claim to fame."

- Let him hear you thank God for him.

JERRY SOLOMON
From *Marriage, Family, and Sexuality*

And now these three remain:

faith, hope and love.

But the greatest of these is love.

PAUL THE APOSTLE

In dreams and love

there are no impossibilities.

JANOS ARANY

The question is asked, "Can there be anything

more beautiful than young love?" Yes, there is

a more beautiful thing than young love.

Old love.

AUTHOR UNKNOWN

Loving Little Things for Husbands to Do

- Say "I love you" several times a day.

- Tell her often she is beautiful.

- Kiss her several times a day.

- Hug her several times a day.

- Put your arm around her often.

- Hold her hand while walking.

- Come up behind her and hug her.

- Always sit by her when possible.

- Rub her feet occasionally.

- Give her a massage occasionally.

- Always help her with chairs and open doors for her.

- Ask her opinion when making decisions.

- Show interest in what she does.

- Take her flowers unexpectedly.

- Plan a surprise night out.

- Ask if there are things you can do for her.

- Communicate with her sexually.

- Show affection in public places.

- Serve her breakfast in bed.

- Train yourself to think of her first.

- Show her you are proud to be her husband.

- Train yourself to be romantic.

- Write a love note on the bathroom mirror.

- Call during the day to say "I love you."

- Always call and tell her if you will be late.

- Let her catch you staring lovingly at her.

- Tell her she is your "greatest claim to fame."

- Let her hear you thank God for her.

JERRY SOLOMON
From *Marriage, Family, and Sexuality*

A Gift for Your Spouse

THE GIFT OF TIME:

*Encouraging her
to spend time doing what
she enjoys most.*

✣

Oh, the comfort, the inexpressible comfort
of feeling safe with another person.

DINAH CRAIK

Few delights can equal
the mere presence of one whom
we trust utterly.

GEORGE MACDONALD

To see a young couple loving each other
is no wonder, but to see an old couple loving
each other is the best sight of all.

WILLIAM M. THACKERAY

Five Principles for Authentic Communication

1. Communication problems are usually heart problems.

2. Your ears are your most important communication tools.

3. Good communication doesn't happen by accident.

4. The absence of conflict doesn't equal good communication.

5. Motive is more important than technique.

JOSHUA HARRIS
Condensed from *Boy Meets Girl*

What Prevents Us from Communicating More?

When we...

- don't know what to say.

- feel that we don't have anything worthwhile to say.

- are afraid of starting a fight.

- are concerned about sounding foolish.

- don't know how to put thoughts and feelings into the right words.

- think it will take too much effort.

- don't feel like our partner will truly listen.

- are too busy to talk.

- are afraid of being too vulnerable.

- believe "talking will get you into trouble."

DR. STEVE STEPHENS
Adapted from *Understanding the One You Love*

12 Actions for a Successful Marriage

Ask

Listen

Accept

Respect

Risk

Encourage

Adjust

Forgive

Give

Love

Laugh

Comfort

Reigniting the Romance after Age 50

In our national survey on long-term marriage, we discovered that
sexual satisfaction actually goes up, not down, for those married
thirty-plus years. So how can you reignite the spark?

- BE AFFECTIONATE

    Romance isn't reserved just for the bedroom. Being affection-
    ate, thoughtful, and kind at other times will spill into your
    love life. Phone calls, notes, holding hands, a peck on the
    cheek, a wink across the room—all will add romance
    to your relationship.

- BE A LISTENER

    Two of the most important lovemaking skills and romance
    enhancers are listening with your heart and talking to your
    spouse.

- BE ADVENTURESOME

  Try a little spontaneity. Explore.

- BE PLAYFUL

  Romance depends on your attitude and perspective.

- GET IN SHAPE

  Get enough exercise. Eat right and get enough sleep. An annual physical is a good investment in the health of your marriage.

- BE A LITTLE WACKY

  What can you do to jolt you out of your old patterns? Plan a getaway and kidnap your wife. Or surprise your wife by coming home early or by taking a morning off and staying home together.

DAVID AND CLAUDIA ARP
From *New Man* magazine

How to Make Your Bedroom More Romantic

○ *The sense of sight:*

Unclutter. Add candles and flowers and a string of small,

white twinkle lights.

○ *The sense of sound:*

Gather your most romantic tapes or compact discs and relax.

○ *The sense of smell:*

Air out and freshen up your room. Use scented candles.

Wear your favorite perfume or cologne.

○ *The sense of taste:*

Have chocolate and/or fruit. Add sparkling cider.

○ *The sense of touch:*

Satin sheets and pillows add comfort.

Use massage oil and give each other back rubs.

BILL AND PAM FARRELL
A very romantic couple

Nine Ways to E-N-C-O-U-R-A-G-E Each Other

Express love.

Nurture your relationship.

Cooperate with each other.

Observe ways to creatively demonstrate love.

Understand—don't lecture.

Remember your blessings.

Accept each other.

Grow together.

Enjoy each other.

DUANE STORY AND SANFORD KULKIN
From *Body and Soul*

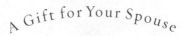

A Gift for Your Spouse

THE GIFT OF COMMITMENT:

*Standing beside her through
thick and thin, sickness and health,
good times and bad.*

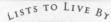

50 Habits for Marriage

1. Start each day with a kiss.

2. Wear your wedding ring at all times.

3. Date once a week.

4. Accept differences.

5. Be polite.

6. Be gentle.

7. Give gifts.

8. Smile often.

9. Touch.

10. Talk about dreams.

11. Choose a song that can be "your song."

12. Give back rubs.

13. Laugh together.

14. Send a card for no reason.

15. Do what she wants before she asks.

16. Listen.

17. Encourage.

18. Do it his way.

19. Know her needs.

20. Fix his favorite breakfast.

21. Compliment her twice a day.

22. Call him.

23. Slow down.

24. Hold hands.

25. Cuddle.

26. Ask her opinion.

27. Show respect.

28. Welcome her home.

29. Look your best for him.

30. Wink at her.

31. Celebrate birthdays in a big way.

32. Apologize.

33. Forgive.

34. Set up a romantic getaway.

35. Ask, "What can I do to make you happier?"

36. Be positive.

37. Be kind.

38. Be vulnerable.

39. Respond quickly to his requests.

40. Talk about your love.

41. Reminisce about your favorite times together.

42. Treat her friends and relatives with courtesy.

43. Send flowers every Valentine's Day and anniversary.

44. Admit when you are wrong.

45. Be sensitive to his sexual desires.

46. Pray for her daily.

47. Watch sunsets together.

48. Say "I love you" frequently.

49. End each day with a hug.

50. Seek outside help when you need it.

DR. STEVE STEPHENS
From *Understanding the One You Love*

A Gift for Your Spouse

THE GIFT OF HUMILITY:

*Admitting that you
are not always right and
being willing to change
where needed.*

Why Is a Healthy Marriage So Important?

1. It teaches love.

2. It conquers loneliness.

3. It nurtures children.

4. It builds character.

True Love . . .

- ○ Shows a daily commitment to each other's happiness.

- ○ Wants to do what the other enjoys.

- ○ Grants space when needed.

- ○ Knows the other's weaknesses and doesn't mention them.

- ○ Celebrates the other's strengths.

- ○ Shares feelings with honesty and sensitivity.

- ○ Demonstrates trustworthiness.

- ○ Believes the best of each other.

❦

*Let the wife make the
husband glad to come home,
and let him make her sorry
to see him leave.*

MARTIN LUTHER

*Love one another deeply,
from the heart.*

PETER THE APOSTLE

*Love comforteth
like sunshine after rain.*

WILLIAM SHAKESPEARE

Strategies for the Second Half of Marriage

Let go of past marital disappointments,
forgive each other, and commit to making
the rest of your marriage the best.

Create a marriage that is partner-focused
rather than child-focused.

Maintain effective communication that allows
you to express your deepest feelings, joys, and concerns.

Use anger and conflict creatively
to build your relationship.

Build a deeper friendship
and enjoy your spouse.

Renew romance and restore
a pleasurable sexual relationship.

Adjust to changing roles with
aging parents and adult children.

Evaluate where you are
on your spiritual pilgrimage.

DAVID AND CLAUDIA ARP
Condensed from *The Second Half of Marriage*

How Well Do We Communicate?

1. Both of us are available to listen when one of us wants to talk.

2. Both of us are sympathetic and understanding when either of us wants to share deeper feelings.

3. Neither of us has to weigh our words carefully to keep the other from getting angry or upset.

4. Both of us usually have interesting things to talk about with each other.

5. Both of us are generally satisfied with our efforts to please one another sexually, including open conversation about sex.

6. Both of us see our partner as our best friend and feel free to share our hurts and frustrations, even when we don't agree.

7. Both of us generally do not interrupt each other.

8. Both of us make special effort not to belittle or put down each other in front of other people.

9. Neither of us has a habit of criticizing or correcting the other.

10. Each of us helps the other feel good about ourselves and lets the other know how valuable and important we are to the other.

11. Each of us understands and respects the other's desire for occasional privacy and times to be alone.

12. Neither of us hesitates to apologize when we have offended the other.

13. Both of us find ease in discussing our spiritual life together.

14. Both of us are sensitive to the emotional support we each desire and need.

FLORENCE AND FRED LITTAUER
Adapted from *After Every Wedding Comes a Marriage*

How to Mismanage Conflict

Avoid

Threaten

Dig up the past

Blame

Belittle

Explode

Manipulate

Try to win rather than understand

Refuse to make up

How to Manage Conflict

1. Keep short accounts. This serves to minimize the pent-up emotions that lead to anger.

2. Think before you speak. If you dump the whole emotional load first, without thinking, you'll spend more time than you care to imagine cleaning up the mess.

3. Describe how you feel. Preferably in a controlled tone of voice; you're likely to create a cooler atmosphere.

4. Seek resolution quickly. Anger left to fester becomes a deep emotional infection that only gets worse as time passes.

H. DALE BURKE
Condensed from *A Love That Never Fails*

A Gift for Your Spouse

THE GIFT OF HONESTY:

Being totally open and honest

and not keeping secrets.

Seven Resolutions for Your Marriage

1. Never purposely hurt each other.

2. Let go of past hurts.

3. Apologize when needed.

4. Support each other in public.

5. Praise each other to family and friends.

6. Look your best for each other.

7. Never use the word divorce.

20 Ways to Make Your Wife Feel Special

1. Ask her to dance when you hear your love song.

2. Polish her shoes for special occasions.

3. Have good conversation when you'd rather read the paper.

4. Give her a back rub with no expectations of lovemaking.

5. Buy and plant a rosebush as a surprise.

6. Keep your home repaired and in good order.

7. Make sure the car has good tires and is in good running condition.

8. Hold her hand when you lead the family in prayer.

9. Write out a list of all your important documents and where you keep them.

10. Find a way to save something from every paycheck.

11. Ask her input before making decisions.

12. Hold her tenderly when she cries, and tell her it's okay.

13. Ask her out and plan the entire date yourself, including making the reservations.

14. Occasionally, eat quiche and dainty desserts with her at a Victorian restaurant.

15. Understand when she forgets to enter a check in the ledger.

16. Shave on your day off.

17. Call if you're going to be more than fifteen minutes late.

18. Encourage her to take time out with her friends.

19. Remember to carry a clean handkerchief when you go to a romantic movie.

20. Tell her she will always be beautiful when she worries about getting older.

AL GRAY
Married thirty-four years

20 Ways to Make Your Husband Feel Special

1. Don't interrupt or correct him when he is telling a story.

2. Compliment him in front of his children, your parents, his parents, and friends.

3. Be as concerned about your looks as you were when you were dating.

4. Let him have some time to relax when he arrives home from work.

5. Develop a genuine interest in his work and hobbies.

6. Admire him for his strength and significance.

7. If he wants to take a lunch to work, pack it for him.

8. Try to be home (and off the phone) when he gets home from work and up in the morning when he leaves.

9. Help your kids be excited about Dad coming home.

10. Buy him new socks and underwear on ordinary days instead of giving them as gifts on holidays or birthdays.

11. Keep your bedroom tastefully decorated and clutter free.

12. Understand when he wants to spend time enjoying sports or hobbies with his friends.

13. Keep his favorite snack on hand.

14. Stick to your budget.

15. Watch his favorite sport events with him.

16. Try to go to bed at the same time he does, and understand if he falls asleep in the recliner after a hard day.

17. Trade baby-sitting with friends so you have some nights at home alone.

18. Keep lovemaking fresh and exciting, and remember that he probably has more frequent desires than you have.

19. Bake homemade cookies for him to take to work.

20. Ask *yourself* one question every day: "What's it like being married to me?"

ALICE GRAY
From her seminar *Three Treasures for Every Marriage*

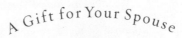

A Gift for Your Spouse

THE GIFT OF ATTENTION:

Listening to what he says

and taking it seriously.

⁂

*We are shaped and
fashioned by what we love.*

GOETHE

*Marriage is not so much
finding the right person as
being the right person.*

CHARLES W. SHEDD

*Grow old along with me!
The best is yet to be,
The last of life for which
the first was made.*

ROBERT BROWNING

Between a Husband and Wife

- We provide emotional, physical, and spiritual safety.

- We promise unconditional love and acceptance.

- We say in a hundred ways, "We belong together, here!"

- We provide for, and are sensitive to, each other's needs.

- We're loyal to each other—against all rumor and criticism, in the face of failure, in spite of disappointments.

DAVID AND HEATHER KOPP
Condensed from *Unquenchable Love*

A Regret-Free Marriage

1. Refuse to divorce.

2. Make your mate's happiness a priority.

3. Avoid hurtful words with your mate.

4. Build memories with your mate.

ROBERT JEFFRESS
From *Say Goodbye to Regret*

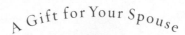

A Gift for Your Spouse

THE GIFT OF CARING:

*Doing my best to know
and meet her emotional needs.*

What Makes Marriage Worthwhile?

- "Our friendship and the ability to work together on common goals."

- "Strong communication skills. And we build each other up constantly."

- "We are best friends and really enjoy being together."

- "Spiritual commitment and commitment to each other."

- "Companionship and sexual fulfillment."

- "Mutual commitment and faith in God."

- "We love each other and are best friends who inspire each other and stand together through the difficult times."

- "We like each other, we let each other be ourselves, and we work together well."

- "The support we give to each other during the good times and the not-so-good times."

- "Humor, love, worship, sex."

- "Laughter and the fun we have together."

- "Solid love and determination to make it work through the good and the bad."

- "There is never a dull moment."

DAVID AND CLAUDIA ARP
Condensed from *The Second Half of Marriage*

Ten Suggestions for Touching

1. Show each other where you like to be touched and the kind of touch that pleases you. Usually, a light touch is the most thrilling. Be imaginative in the way you caress.

2. Demonstrate to each other how you prefer to be held. Kiss your partner the way you would like to be kissed—not to criticize past performances, but to communicate something your partner has not sensed before.

3. To learn the art of expressing warm, sensual feelings, you will have to slow down. If what you are doing feels good, take the time to enjoy it.

4. Caress each other's backs. Pay special attention to the back of the neck at the hairline and the area just above the small of the back.

5. Make sure that both of you have equal opportunity to give and to receive. Take turns giving pleasure to each other.

6. Have a period of fifteen to thirty minutes every night to lie in each other's arms in the dark before you drift off to sleep. Whisper together, sharing private thoughts and pleasant little experiences of the day. This is the time to build intimacy and wind down for sleep.

7. Establish the cozy habit of staying in some sort of physical contact while you are going to sleep—a hand or a leg touching your partner's, for instance.

8. Begin every day with a few minutes of cuddling and snuggling before you get out of bed. A husband can tell his wife how nice she feels and how glad he is to be close to her. A wife can

nestle in her husband's arms and tell him she wishes they didn't have to leave each other that morning. Just be close and savor gentle physical contact for a while.

9. Hold hands often. Think of all the different ways you can enjoy just touching with your hands and all the different feelings that can be conveyed.

10. Become aware of the many ways you can have physical contact in the course of a week. Touch when you are talking and maintain eye contact. Sit close to each other in church. Kiss each other when there is no occasion for it. Add variety to your kisses, your touches, and your love pats.

ED WHEAT, M.D.
Condensed from *Love Life for Every Married Couple*

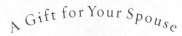

A Gift for Your Spouse

THE GIFT OF FORGIVENESS:

Forgiving him,

getting over it, and not

bringing it up again.

What Would Improve Your Sexual Relations?

Gentle initiation

Increased frequency

Increased touching

Increased cuddling

More romance

Longer foreplay

More variety

Better communication

Better hygiene

Increased passion

Romantic atmosphere
(music, candlelight, perfume)

Increased patience

Different time of day

DR. STEVE STEPHENS
From *Understanding the One You Love*

A Gift for Your Spouse

THE GIFT OF RESPECT:

Treating her with courtesy

in both word and deed.

Tips for the Romantically Challenged

1. *Shower Her with Praise.* Praise not only affects her; it changes your perception of her.

2. *Try New Things.* Boredom is a mortal enemy to relationships.

3. *Establish Rituals.* Romantic rituals ensure that you are spending quality time together on a regular basis. If you wait until you are feeling spontaneous or "in the mood" to be romantic, you may end up waiting a long time.

4. *Get Away!* Don't make the mistake of thinking you can't afford to take time away—you can't afford not to!

MICHAEL WEBB
Condensed from *New Man* magazine

50 Fun Things to Do with Your Spouse

1. Look at picture albums.

2. Have a candlelight dinner.

3. Give each other fifteen-minute back rubs.

4. Make a date for a concert or a play.

5. Listen to your favorite recording.

6. Take a short walk.

7. Go window shopping.

8. Tell each other two jokes.

9. Write a poem to each other.

10. Go to a movie.

11. Play charades.

12. Buy a plant.

13. Read a book, story, or article together.

14. Plan a trip to the zoo.

15. Sing some songs together.

16. Bake cookies together (clean up together, too).

17. Make a surprise visit to someone.

18. Go bowling.

19. Make valentines for each other.

20. Read Song of Solomon.

21. Play hide-and-seek.

22. Talk about favorite memories.

23. Go camping (at a campground or in the backyard).

24. Go bicycle riding.

25. Have a wiener roast.

26. Call your spouse just to say "I love you."

27. Send flowers for no special reason.

28. Call and invite your spouse to lunch.

29. Put a love note where your spouse can find it.

30. Make popcorn or fudge.

31. Tell each other bedtime stories.

32. Go for a scenic drive.

33. Act out a play or skit with each other.

34. Plan a trip to the beach.

35. Spend a day in the city.

36. Surprise the other with dinner reservations.

37. Spend a night at a motel (or hotel).

38. Play a favorite board game.

39. Spend an afternoon hiking.

40. Finger paint.

41. Go on a picnic.

42. Play racquetball or tennis.

43. Go out for breakfast.

44. Work in the yard together.

45. Wash the car.

46. Have a pillow fight.

47. Make love by candlelight.

48. Take a class together.

49. Spend an evening in front of the fireplace.

50. Attend a sporting event.

Your Best Friend

A friend sees the best in you even when you're not showing it.

A friend knows when you need someone to talk to
and when you need to be alone—and most importantly,
the difference between the two.

A friend can tell when you need a hug and
doesn't hesitate to offer one.

A friend makes you laugh
when you can see little to laugh about.

A friend will always come to your defense, no matter
how often called upon or how unpopular it makes him.

A friend believes you first and rumors second.

A friend never passes up the chance to encourage you.

A friend shares with you (even chocolate).

A friend tells you when you're about to make a mistake.

A friend is someone you can always depend on,
even when you don't deserve it.

A friend brings out the best in you
but doesn't insist on the credit.

A friend understands you even when you don't.

A friend makes the best spouse.

MARTHA BOLTON
From *I Love You…Still*

How to Be Happy in Marriage

If you will be happy in marriage—

Confide

Love

Be patient

Be faithful

Be firm

Be holy

MARTIN F. TUPPER
Nineteenth-century philosopher

A Gift for Your Spouse

THE GIFT OF ENCOURAGEMENT:

Looking for opportunities

to compliment him and

build him up.

Doing It Together

Walk along the beach.

Read a great book.

Enjoy a sunset.

Laugh until it hurts.

Listen to romantic music.

Snuggle in front of a fire.

Watch your favorite video.

Cook a meal.

Help someone in need.

Grow old together.

Trust Builders

1. Showing others how proud you are of your spouse.

2. Keeping your word.

3. Making your spouse a priority.

4. Knowing when your spouse is stressed and doing what you can to reduce it.

5. Being dependable.

6. Never forgetting your anniversary.

7. Giving each other space when needed and closeness the rest of the time.

8. Always wearing your wedding ring.

Trust Busters

1. Keeping secrets from each other.

2. Not being honest.

3. Flirting with someone else.

4. Embarrassing your spouse.

5. Breaking promises.

6. Being critical.

7. Lack of follow-through.

8. Not showing complete, unselfish, committed love.

13 Rules for Fighting Fair

1. Make an appointment for the discussion.

2. Face each other.

3. Keep it limited to one issue.

4. Keep it respectful.

5. Remain focused on the present.

6. Stay focused on understanding first,

   being understood second.

7. Focus on the problem, not the person.

8. Avoid distractions.

9. Keep it clean.

10. Keep it tactful.

11. Take a time-out if needed.

12. Don't interrupt.

13. Remember that your reality isn't the only reality.

CAROL CLIFTON, PH.D.
Psychologist

Pray for His . . .

Temptations

Work

Faith

Health

Success

Pray for Her . . .

Attitude

Patience

Wisdom

Energy

Contentment

Pray Together for Our . . .

Communication

Togetherness

Love

Understanding

Joy

A Gift for Your Spouse

THE GIFT OF LAUGHTER:

Playing and

having fun together.

Wisdom *for* Marriage

❧

Marriage is our last,
best chance to grow up.

JOSEPH BARTH

A heart that loves is always young.

GREEK PROVERB

A successful marriage
requires falling in love many times,
always with the same person.

MIGNON MCLAUGHLIN

Seven Committments for a Strong Marriage

We Commit to...

1. Oneness in body, spirit, and soul.

2. Positive communication.

3. Quality time together.

4. Growth and improvement of the relationship.

5. Emotional and sexual faithfulness.

6. Honesty.

7. A lifelong love.

What Are Your Dreams?

- What gifts could we give each other that would be most meaningful?

- What could we do for each other that would bring the most joy?

- Where have you always wanted to go but have not gone?

- What have you always wanted to do but have not done?

- If you had just one month to live, how would you like to spend it? What would you want to do? Where would you want to go?

- What would you like me to do to improve our relationship?

- If we were given a million dollars, what would you like to do with the money?

- What could we do to make our relationship more romantic?

- How can I help your dreams come true?

20 Creative, Romantic Ideas That Cost under $20

1. Dress up for a meal you bring back from your favorite fast food restaurant. Take out a tablecloth, centerpiece, and a tape or CD of your favorite romantic music, and dine to a "Golden Arches" delight.

2. Buy a half-gallon of your favorite ice cream, go to the most beautiful park in town, throw a blanket on the ground, and eat every last spoonful of the ice cream.

3. Visit a museum or art gallery. Talk with each other about the art you like and dislike. Concentrate on listening to the other person and learning all you can from what he or she says.

4. Go to a driving range together. Cheer each other's good shots.

5. Go bowling together. Come up with prizes you can give each other for winning games: a massage, a week's worth of doing dishes, a promise to paint the fence, etc.

6. Go on a hayride with four other couples, singing camp songs accompanied by a tape recorder or guitar. Have a cookout under the stars afterward.

7. Write love notes to one another and hide them in unusual places like the freezer, a shoe, the car's glove box, the bathtub, a makeup kit, or under the bedcover.

8. Go snorkeling in a lake.

9. Collect leaves and pine cones together on an autumn day. Take them home and make fall ornaments for the house.

10. Attend a free outdoor concert.

11. Buy a pass from the Forest Service, go to a National Forest, and cut your own Christmas tree.

12. Buy a modern paraphrase of the Song of Solomon, and read it to each other.

13. Walk hand in hand along a nature trail.

14. Watch a sunset together.

15. Make "dough" ornaments together, bake them, and color them with the kids.

16. Rent each other's all-time favorite movies and play a double feature at home.

17. Go to your favorite restaurant for dessert. Bring a child's baby book or your wedding album and relive some memories together.

18. Throw a party commemorating your spouse's graduation date.

19. Get the children together and make a "Why I Love Mom" and "Why I Love Dad" book, complete with text and illustrations.

20. Take your spouse out for an afternoon in her favorite store. Note the items under $20 she likes best. Return to the store the next day and buy one of these items as a gift.

GARY SMALLEY WITH JOHN TRENT
From *Love Is a Decision*

The 20 Most Romantic Gifts

1. Hot-air balloon ride for two

2. Exquisite chocolate with a secret love note

3. RV rental for a weekend getaway

4. Basket of bubble bath, fragrant candles, and champagne with two glasses

5. A Reader Board personalized message

6. Bouquet of flowers delivered

7. Two-hour canoe rental

8. Written invitation for dinner at a favorite restaurant

9. Silk sheets

10. Horseback ride on the beach

11. Framed photo of the two of you

12. Car ride with a surprise picnic lunch

13. Picture of a bed-and-breakfast with the words, "When shall we go?"

14. Love poem placed inside a fortune cookie or seashell

15. Weekend to a hot springs, mountain lodge, or lakeside cabin

16. An engraved piece of jewelry with a personalized message

17. Art piece selected together

18. Sleigh, carriage, or cable car ride

19. Lingerie gift certificate

20. A personalized CD with your favorite love song

DEBORAH WESTENDORF
President, The Hen's Tooth, Inc.

A Gift for Your Spouse

THE GIFT OF GENEROSITY:

*Showing her your love
by giving time, words, things,
and memories.*

True Love Is . . .

- Love at the greatest point of pain.

- Love at the greatest point of vulnerability.

- Love at the greatest point of failure.

DR. GARY AND BARB ROSBERG
Condensed from *The 5 Love Needs of Men and Women*

Wisdom *for* Marriage

❧

May you rejoice in the wife of your youth....
May you ever be captivated by her love.

KING SOLOMON

Henceforth there will be such a oneness between us—
that when one weeps the other will taste salt.

AUTHOR UNKNOWN

If I had a single flower for
every time I think about you,
I could walk forever in my garden.

CLAUDIA GRANDE

Are You a Great Marriage Partner?

1. Do you give your spouse a hug or kiss each morning?

2. Do you look for opportunities to express your love?

3. Do you surprise your spouse with compliments and gifts?

4. Do you let go of passing annoyances or differences that could turn into conflicts?

5. Do you periodically do it his way?

6. Do you take the time to have heart-to-heart chats?

7. Do you truly listen to her?

8. Do you sometimes say "I'm sorry"?

9. Do you allow your spouse to "lose it" every once in a while?

10. Do you pray for each other regularly?

11. Do you show your love even when you don't feel like it?

12. Do you have eyes only for your partner?

13. Do you share your dreams and talk about how you can make them come true?

14. Do you expect to love and cherish him "for as long as you both shall live"?

15. Do you frequently say "I love you"?

Four Promises of Forgiveness

- I will no longer dwell on this incident.

- I will not bring up this incident again and use it against you.

- I will not talk to others about this incident.

- I will not allow this incident to stand between us
  or hinder our relationship.

KEN SANDE
From *The Peacemaker*

Six Steps Toward Reconciliation

1. Guard your attitudes.

2. Avoid or abandon any romantic relationship with another adult.

3. Realize that divorce will not lead to personal happiness.

4. Understand that your marital difficulty is caused by the marriage partners, not by someone outside the marriage. Therefore, each partner must work toward reconciliation.

5. Do not date during the separation period.

6. Move slowly in completing any legal separation papers.

DR. GARY CHAPMAN
From *Hope for the Separated*

21 Things Every Couple Should Know

- The qualities within your spouse that ignited your interest when you first met.

- How to give your spouse a visible expression of love.

- The importance of looking into your spouse's eyes while listening.

- One compliment a day isn't too many.

- Good memories are priceless no matter what they cost.

- The importance of courtship after marriage.

- How to make your spouse laugh.

- The simple intimacy of holding hands.

- A romantic location within walking distance from your home.

- Unexpected gifts can bring great pleasure.

- Marriages are built on small expressions of affection.

- How to appreciate and accept the differences in your partner.

- How to say "I'm sorry."

- How to agree more and argue less.

- Being the right person is more important than trying to change your spouse into the right person.

- How to make every anniversary a special celebration.

- A growing marriage gets stronger and better over the years.

- Guidelines for a great marriage won't work unless you apply them.

- The triggers that hurt feelings.

- The value of a hug.

- Your spouse is priceless.

DOUG FIELDS

Selected from *365 Things Every Couple Should Know*

Talk about How You Want to Spend These Holidays

Birthdays

Wedding Anniversary

Christmas or Hanukkah

New Year's Eve

Valentine's Day

Easter

Mother's Day

Father's Day

A Gift for Your Spouse

THE GIFT OF FRIENDSHIP:

Being the best friend I can be.

Talk about Your Expectations in These Areas

Romance

Finances

Fitness

Career

Education

Friendships

Recreation

Faith

In-laws

Children

Pets

Sharing household chores

Hobbies

Holidays and vacations

How to Make Your Marriage Healthy

1. COMMITMENT

   True commitment means much more than simply committing to staying married. Genuine commitment involves being committed to the growth and best interest of your partner.

2. TEAMWORK

   Use the five important words in marriage: "Let's try it your way."

3. COMMUNICATION

   Without exception, every couple I have ever worked with struggles with effective communication. Part of the reason is that two people with the exact same communication style rarely marry each other.

4. MEETING EMOTIONAL NEEDS

   Discover and then meet the emotional needs of your partner. How? Simple: just ask!

5. RESOLVING CONFLICT

Conflict in marriage is inevitable. Fighting is optional.

6. APOLOGY & FORGIVENESS

On a regular basis, practice the three A's of successful relationships: *Apologize* for something from the past, *appreciate* something in the present, and *anticipate* something in the future.

7. CREATING A RELATIONSHIP VISION

Ask yourselves and each other this question: "If we knew we couldn't fail, and if we could design our relationship any way we wanted it, how would we like to be?"

JEFF HERRING
From the *Oregonian*

His Needs, Her Needs

THE MAN'S MOST BASIC NEEDS:

1. Sexual fulfillment

2. Recreational companionship

3. Honesty and openness

4. Domestic support

5. Admiration

THE WOMAN'S MOST BASIC NEEDS:

1. Affection

2. Conversation

3. An attractive spouse

4. Financial support

5. Family commitment

Time and again these ten needs have surfaced as I have helped literally thousands of couples improve their troubled marriages. Although each individual may perceive his or her needs differently, the consistency with which these two sets of five categories have surfaced to explain marital problems impresses me.

WILLARD HARLEY
Condensed from
His Needs, Her Needs: Basic Needs in Marriage

20 Most Romantic Literary Works

1. *Romeo and Juliet,* William Shakespeare

2. *Jane Eyre,* Charlotte Brontë

3. *Emma,* Jane Austen

4. *A Severe Mercy,* Sheldon Van Auken

5. *Gone with the Wind,* Margaret Mitchell

6. *The Gift of the Magi,* O. Henry

7. *Don Quixote,* Miguel de Cervantes

8. *Anna Karenina,* Leo Tolstoy

9. *Wuthering Heights,* Emily Brontë

10. *Green Dolphin Street,* Elizabeth Goudge

11. *Dr. Zhivago,* Boris Pasternak

12. *Two-Part Invention*, Madeleine L'Engle

13. *Still by Your Side*, Marjorie Holmes

14. *The Story of the Trapp Family Singers*, Maria Augusta Trapp [basis for *The Sound of Music*]

15. *Spartacus*, Howard Fast

16. *Ben-Hur*, Lew Wallace

17. *The Girl of the Limberlost*, Gene Stratton Porter

18. *Pygmalion*, George Bernard Shaw [basis for *My Fair Lady*]

19. *Sonnets from the Portuguese*, Elizabeth Barrett Browning

20. *Song of Solomon*, King Solomon

DAVID KOPP AND HEATHER HARPHAM KOPP
Authors of *Love Stories God Told*

20 Most Romantic Songs

1. *Unforgettable,* Nat King Cole

2. *Wonderful World,* Louis Armstrong

3. *I Only Have Eyes for You,* The Flamingos

4. *When a Man Loves a Woman,* Percy Sledge

5. *Let's Stay Together,* Al Green

6. *My Heart Will Go On* (theme from *Titanic*), Celine Dion

7. *You Are So Beautiful,* Joe Cocker

8. *Love Me Tender,* Elvis

9. *The Way We Were,* Barbara Streisand

10. *I Will Always Love You,* Whitney Houston

11. *Crazy,* Patsy Cline

12. *Wedding Song* (There Is Love), Paul Stookey

13. *Your Song,* Elton John

14. *As Time Goes By,* Jimmy Durante

15. *Strangers in the Night,* Frank Sinatra

16. *All I Have to Do Is Dream,* The Everly Brothers

17. *Some Enchanted Evening,* from the musical *South Pacific*

18. *Always,* composed by Irving Berlin

19. *Where Do I Begin?* (theme from *Love Story*)

20. *Moonlight Serenade,* Glenn Miller

KYLE LIEDTKE, MUSIC DIRECTOR
KNLR-FM, Bend, Oregon

Ten Greatest Romance Movies

1. An Affair to Remember

2. Beauty and the Beast (1940)

3. Casablanca

4. Doctor Zhivago

5. Gone with the Wind

6. Roman Holiday

7. Shadowlands

8. Somewhere in Time

9. Return to Me

10. Wuthering Heights

COMPILED BY DAN MCAULEY
Longtime movie buff

How to Love Him Unconditionally

1. Show grace with his weakness.

2. Affirm him whenever you can.

3. Help him feel safe.

4. Take time to connect.

5. Study him.

GARY ROSBERG
Condensed from
The 5 Love Needs of Men and Women

How to Love Her Unconditionally

1. Encourage her.

2. Stand with her.

3. Compliment her.

4. Respect her opinion.

5. Talk with her—and listen.

6. Be tender with her.

7. Spend time with her.

8. Serve her.

BARBARA ROSBERG
Condensed from
The 5 Love Needs of Men and Women

Daily Tips for Your Marriage

1.

Verbally share the events of the day.

2.

Renew statements regarding the relationship.

"I love you."

"You are special to me."

"I missed you."

"I have been looking forward to being with you."

3.

Touch each other in meaningful ways—
hugs, kisses, holding hands, sitting close.

4.

Remember that commitment leads to communication;
communication stimulates forgiveness;
forgiveness offers grace, which develops intimacy.

5.

Show appreciation for something your partner has done—
say thank you.

6.

Take turns asking and explaining
when you have misunderstood each other.

7.

Share hopes and dreams—a basic to a close relationship.

8.

Be a good listener—no response may be necessary.

GLENDA HOTTON, M.A.
Counselor

A Gift for Your Spouse

THE GIFT OF DREAMS:

*Planning the future together
with the commitment that you will spend
the rest of your days side by side.*

When the Situation Is Difficult, Ask...

- How can we benefit from this situation?

- How should we deal with the situation in a positive way?

- How can we use this to strengthen our marriage?

- What can we do or say to alleviate each other's fears, allowing us to communicate openly and honestly?

- How can we encourage each other?

DUANE STORY AND SANFORD KULKIN
From *Body and Soul*

Suggestions on How to Serve Your Spouse

1. Admit to your spouse that you have made mistakes and that you desire to change.

2. Ask your spouse to tell you one thing that you could either begin doing or stop doing to make life easier or more meaningful.

3. Write your spouse's suggestions on a card or a poster for future reference.

4. Ask God to help you serve your spouse better.

5. Continue to ask for suggestions, building them into your lifestyle. This will require thought, prayer, and discipline, but the satisfaction of genuinely serving your spouse is worth the effort.

GARY CHAPMAN
From *Decision* magazine

Love . . .

- Is very patient

- Is kind

- Is never jealous

- Is never envious

- Is never boastful

- Is never proud

- Is never haughty

- Is never selfish

- Is never rude

- Does not demand its own way

- Is not irritable or touchy

- Does not hold grudges

- Will hardly even notice when others do it wrong

- Is never glad about injustice

- Rejoices whenever truth wins out

- Is loyal no matter what the cost

- Will always believe

- Will always expect the best

- Will always defend

- Goes on forever

PAUL THE APOSTLE
Condensed from 1 Corinthians 13:4–8

Ten Reasons Divorce Isn't the Answer

1. It rarely solves the problem.

2. It is a financial disaster.

3. It blocks personal growth and maturity.

4. It sets you up to repeat your difficulty
   with someone else.

5. It hardens your heart.

6. It weakens your faith.

7. It increases your loneliness.

8. It devastates your children.

9. It hurts friends and relatives.

10. It impacts your legacy.

20 Marriage Memories

Love letters. Find the first love letters and notes of affection you sent each other. Mount them on red paper and draw pink and red hearts around the page with a photo-safe pen.

Your wedding invitation. Mount the invitation to your special day on colored paper that matches your wedding theme.

Newspaper announcements of your wedding, anniversaries, and family births. Copy the announcements on acid-free paper so you won't have yellowing newspapers in your scrapbook.

Family holiday picture. Take a photo each year in front of your Christmas tree or fireplace or in your yard. Mount each photo on red and green paper; be sure to write the year under each picture.

Vacation postcards. Create a montage with the postcards; don't forget to include the dates of your trips.

Piece of fabric from your wedding dress. Mount it inside a photo-safe sleeve. You can also include fabric from your bridesmaids' dresses or a birdseed ribbon or candy favor from your wedding day.

Your song. Find the words to "your" song and mount them on black paper; add musical note stickers.

Photo of your first house or apartment. Mount the photo with coordinating colored paper. Write down your thoughts and feelings about your first home.

Receipts. Create a page with receipts from your honeymoon, first mortgage payment, first car purchase, grocery bills, etc. Then include similar receipts from fifteen, twenty, or thirty years later.

Christmas card. Mount a sample of the Christmas card you send each year on your scrapbook page or place it in a photo album pocket page.

Tickets and programs. Mount ticket stubs and programs from your favorite plays, concerts, or sporting events; then add your own review or special memory of the event.

Books, movies, and songs. Make lists of the books, movies, and songs you have enjoyed together; then mount them on colored paper.

Family generations photo. Take a photo with as many family members as possible. Mount it; then write out your family tree on the opposite page.

Pet photos. Cats, dogs, fish, guinea pigs, maybe even the frog you had for one day. Cut some of the photos out to look like paw prints; write the story of how you got your pet and how much he or she means to your family.

Traditions. Make a list of your favorite traditions. Write it in calligraphy or other fancy printing.

Bible quote or verse. Write out a Bible verse or quotation that has inspired or encouraged both of you. Explain why it has meaning.

Photos, of course! Snapshots of you and your spouse making timeless memories during vacations, holidays, fun times with your kids, and other favorite activities.

Special cards from family and friends sent for your wedding, birthday, anniversary, or "just because." Place them in photo pocket pages so you can remove them and read them again.

ANGELA DEAN LUND
Creative Memories Consultant

Talk about These Things

- What do you think of when you imagine intimacy and closeness?

- What is romance to you? Do you need romance to set the mood for sex?

- What are the positive factors about your love life?

- What brings you the most sexual fulfillment? What do you think brings your partner the most sexual fulfillment?

- How often would you like to make love?

- How much hugging and cuddling do you need before and after intercourse? Define this in minutes if necessary.

- What are the fantasies you have been hoping to fulfill with each other?

- What changes do you need to make to keep sex fresh and growing?

DAVID AND CLAUDIA ARP
Adapted from *Love Life for Parents* and *10 Great Dates*

Springboards to Deeper Conversation

1. What is the happiest thing that has ever happened to you?

2. What has been the hardest experience of your life?

3. What are your secret ambitions—your goals for your life?

4. What are your deepest fears?

5. What about me do you appreciate the most?

6. What traits of mine would you like to see changed?

7. What people do you most admire?

CAROLE MAYHALL
Condensed from *Lord, Teach Me Wisdom*

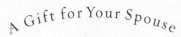

A Gift for Your Spouse

THE GIFT OF CARING:

*Doing my best to know
and meet her emotional needs.*

How to Be an Affectionate Husband

1. Hug and kiss your wife every morning while you are still in bed.

2. Tell her you love her while you're having breakfast together.

3. Kiss her before you leave for work.

4. Call her during the day to see how she is doing.

5. Bring her flowers once in a while as a surprise (be sure to include a card that expresses your love for her).

6. Gifts for special occasions (birthdays, anniversary, Christmas, Mother's Day, and Valentine's Day) should be sentimental, not practical. Learn how to shop for a woman.

7. After work, call her before you leave for home so she can know when to expect you.

8. When you arrive home from work, give her a hug and kiss and spend a few minutes talking to her about how her day went.

9. Help with the dishes after dinner.

10. Hug and kiss her every night before you both go to sleep.

WILLARD HARLEY
From *His Needs, Her Needs*

How to Find the Perfect Gift

- What has she asked for?

- What does he need?

- What does she talk about?

- What does he look at?

- What does she look good in?

- What does he enjoy?

- What has she enjoyed doing in the past?

- What are his hobbies and interests?

- What does she collect?

- Where does he like to go?

- What helps her relax?

- What does he dream of?

TAMI STEPHENS
A sensitive shopper

Wedding Anniversary Gifts

1st — Paper or clocks

2nd — Cotton or china

3rd — Leather or glass

4th — Flowers or small appliances

5th — Wood or silverware

6th — Iron or candy

7th — Wool or copper

8th — Bronze or linen

9th — Pottery or leather

10th — Aluminum or diamond

11th — Steel or jewelry

12th — Silk or pearls

13th — Lace or textiles

14th — Ivory or gold jewelry

15th — Crystal or watches

20th — China or platinum

25th — Silver

30th — Pearl

35th — Coral or jade

40th — Ruby

45th — Sapphire

50th — Gold

55th — Emerald

60th — Diamond

75th — Diamond

Faith Affirmations for a Husband

I will hold my wife close to my heart.

I will protect her.

I will praise her publicly.

I will compliment her.

I will trust and treasure her.

I will listen to her.

I will always be faithful.

I will never abuse or abandon her.

I will love her night and day.

I will grow old with her.

Selected from *The Holy Bible*

Faith Affirmations for a Wife

I will stand beside my husband.

I will be trustworthy.

I will enrich his life.

I will appreciate him and all he does.

I will take care of his needs.

I will yearn deeply for him.

I will share my body with him.

I will cooperate and work with him.

I will love and respect him.

I will hate divorce.

Selected from *The Holy Bible*

Wisdom for Marriage

What greater thing is there for two
human souls than to feel that they are joined…
to strengthen each other…
to be at one with each other in
silent unspeakable memories.

GEORGE ELIOT

Kindness is the life's blood
and elixir of marriage.

RANDOLPH RAY

A happy marriage is the
union of two good forgivers.

ROBERT QUILLEN

Heart-to-Heart

God did not create woman from man's head,

that he should command her,

nor from his feet,

that she should be his slave,

but rather from his side,

that she should be near his heart.

HEBREW PROVERB

Traditional Marriage Vows

For better

or for worse;

For richer

or for poorer;

In sickness

and in health;

To love,

To honor,

To cherish

until death do us part.

Lists for Our Marriage

Promises we want to make for the future...

_____

_____

_____

_____

_____

_____

_____

_____

_____

_____

_____

Lists for Our Marriage

How we can help each other succeed...

_____

_____

_____

_____

_____

_____

_____

_____

_____

_____

_____

Lists for Our Marriage

Things we want to do together...

_____

_____

_____

_____

_____

_____

_____

_____

_____

_____

Lists for Our Marriage

Ways to show we love each other...

_____

_____

_____

_____

_____

_____

_____

_____

_____

_____

_____

Lists for Our Marriage

Things we need to apologize for...

_____

_____

_____

_____

_____

_____

_____

_____

_____

_____

Lists for Our Marriage

Things we need to forgive and let go of...

_____

_____

_____

_____

_____

_____

_____

_____

_____

_____

Lists for Our Marriage

Gifts to give each other...

_____

_____

_____

_____

_____

_____

_____

_____

_____

_____

Life-changing advice
in a quick-to-read format!
LISTS TO LIVE BY

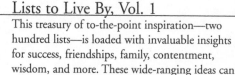

Lists to Live By, Vol. 1

This treasury of to-the-point inspiration—two hundred lists—is loaded with invaluable insights for success, friendships, family, contentment, wisdom, and more. These wide-ranging ideas can change your life!

ISBN 1-57673-478-1

Lists to Live By, Vol. 2

You'll get a lift in a hurry as you browse through this treasure-trove of more *Lists to Live By*—with wisdom for home, health, love, life, faith, and successful living.

ISBN 1-57673-685-7

LISTS TO LIVE BY FOR EVERY CARING FAMILY

compiled by Alice Gray, Steve Stephens, and John Van Diest

Success Strategies of Families that Flourish

Moms and Dads will welcome the loving, insightful, and to-the-point wisdom found in *Lists to Live By for Every Caring Family*. Each of the eighty lists, compiled by three successful and respected authors, offers encouragement and tender advice

for today's parenting challenges. This isn't another trivia book; *Lists* provides new inspiration on how to love, teach, understand, uplift, and communicate with children on topics such as "Helping Your Child Succeed," "Praying for Your Children," and "Four Ways to Encourage Your Kids." Parents will cherish each nugget of truth in this latest timeless collection of *Lists to Live By.*

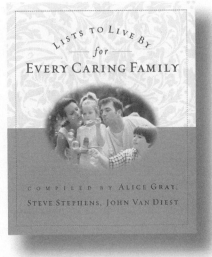

ISBN 1-57673-999-6

Acknowledgments

Hundreds of books and magazines were researched, and dozens of professionals were interviewed for this collection. A diligent effort has been made to attribute original ownership of each list and, when necessary, obtain permission to reprint. If we have overlooked giving proper credit to anyone, please accept our apologies. If you will contact Multnomah Publishers, Inc., Post Office Box 1720, Sisters, Oregon 97759, with written documentation, corrections will be made prior to additional printings.

Notes and acknowledgments in the following bibliography are shown in the order the lists appear in the book. For permission to reprint a list, please request permission from the original source. The editors gratefully acknowledge authors, publishers, and agents who granted permission for reprinting their material.

Lists without attribution were compiled by the editors.

"The Five Love Languages" by Gary Chapman from *The Five Love Languages.* Copyright © 1992. Published by Moody Press. Used by permission.

"Things to Say to Your Spouse" by Dr. Steve Stephens from *Marriage: Experience the Best.* Copyright © 1996. Published by Vision House Publishers, Gresham, OR. Used by permission of the author.

"Things *Not* to Say to Your Spouse" by Dr. Steve Stephens from *Marriage: Experience the Best.* Copyright © 1996. Published by Vision House Publishers, Gresham, OR. Used by permission of the author.

"18 Qualities to Develop in Your Marriage" by Al and Alice Gray, Redmond, Oregon. Used by permission.

"The Top Ten Mistakes Couples Make" written by Marty Crouch. Copyright © Coach U. Used by permission.

"Fun Activities for Couple Friends" by Tricia Goyer condensed from *HomeLife* magazine. Used by permission.

"Bonds of Intimacy" by Ed Wheat, M.D. taken from *Love Life for Every Married Couple* by Ed Wheat and Gloria Okes Perkins. Copyright © 1980, 1987 by Ed Wheat, M.D. Used by permission of Zondervan Publishing House.

"What Is Love?" by Father James Keller, founder "The Christophers" as cited in *More of...The Best of Bits & Pieces*, Rob Gilbert, Ph.D., editor. *More of...The Best of Bits & Pieces* is copyrighted © 1997 by The Economics Press, Inc., 12 Daniel Road, Fairfield, NJ 97004-2565; Phone: 800-526-2554 (US/Canada) or (+1 973) 227-1224 (worldwide). Fax: 973-227-9742 (US/Canada) or (+1 973) 227-9742 (worldwide). E-mail: info@epinc.com. Web site: www.epinc.com Please contact The Economics Press, Inc., directly to purchase this book or for subscription information to the monthly magazine version of *Bits & Pieces*.

"What Draws Us Closer to God?" by Dr. Steve Stephens from *Understanding the One You Love*. Copyright © 1998 by Dr. Steve Stephens. Published by Harvest House Publishers, Eugene, Oregon 97402. Used by permission.

"Don'ts of a Marriage" by Glenda Hotton, M.A., C.D.C., M.F.T. Counselor for Women's Issues of Trauma/Crisis Abuse; Substance Abuse in private practice in Santa Clarita, CA. Used by permission of the author.

"Loving Little Things for Wives to Do" by Jerry Solomon taken from *Marriage, Family, and Sexuality* by Kerby Anderson. Copyright © 2000 Kregel Publications, Grand Rapids, MI. Used by permission. All rights reserved.

"Loving Little Things for Husbands to Do" by Jerry Solomon taken from *Marriage, Family, and Sexuality* by Kerby Anderson. Copyright © 2000 Kregel Publications, Grand Rapids, MI. Used by permission. All rights reserved.

"Five Principles for Authentic Communication" by Joshua Harris condensed from *Boy Meets Girl*. Copyright ©2000, Multnomah Publishers, Inc., Sisters, Oregon. Used by permission.

"What Prevents Us from Communicating More?" by Dr. Steve Stephens from *Understanding the One You Love*. Copyright © 1998 by Dr. Steve

Stephens. Published by Harvest House Publishers, Eugene, Oregon 97402. Used by permission.

"Reigniting the Romance after Age 50" by David and Claudia Arp from *New Man* magazine. Used by permission.

"How to Make Your Bedroom More Romantic" by Bill and Pam Farrell, San Marcos, California. Used by permission of the authors.

"Nine Ways to E-N-C-O-U-R-A-G-E Each Other" by Duane Story and Sanford Kulkin from *Body and Soul*. Copyright © 1998, Multnomah Publishers, Inc., Sisters, Oregon. Used by permission.

"50 Habits for Marriage" by Dr. Steve Stephens from *Understanding the One You Love*. Used by permission of the author.

"Strategies for the Second Half of Marriage" by David and Claudia Arp taken from *The Second Half of Marriage* by David Arp, Claudia Arp. Copyright © 1996 by David and Claudia Arp. Used by permission of Zondervan Publishing House.

"How Well Do We Communicate?" by Florence and Fred Littauer taken from *After Every Wedding Comes a Marriage* by Florence and Fred Littauer. Copyright © 1997 by Harvest House Publishers, Eugene, Oregon 97402. Used by permission.

"How to Manage Conflict" by H. Dale Burke condensed from *A Love That Never Fails*. Copyright © 1999, Moody Press. Used by permission.

"20 Ways to Make Your Wife Feel Special" by Al Gray, Redmond, Oregon. Used by permission of the author.

"20 Ways to Make Your Husband Feel Special" by Alice Gray, Redmond, Oregon. Used by permission of the author.

"Between a Husband and Wife" by David and Heather Kopp taken from *Unquenchable Love* by David and Heather Kopp. Copyright © 1999. Published by Harvest House Publishers, Eugene, Oregon 97402. Used by permission.

"A Regret-Free Marriage" by Robert Jeffress from *Say Goodbye to Regret.* Copyright © 1998, Multnomah Publishers, Inc., Sisters, Oregon. Used by permission.

"What Makes Marriage Worthwhile?" by David and Claudia Arp taken from *The Second Half of Marriage* by David Arp, Claudia Arp. Copyright © 1996 by David and Claudia Arp. Used by permission of Zondervan Publishing House.

"Ten Suggestions for Touching"" by Ed Wheat, M.D. taken from *Love Life for Every Married Couple* by Ed Wheat and Gloria Okes Perkins. Copyright © 1980, 1987 by Ed Wheat, M.D. Used by permission of Zondervan Publishing House.

"What Would Improve Your Sexual Relations?" by Dr. Steve Stephens. Taken from *Understanding the One You Love*. Copyright © 1998 by Dr. Steve

Stephens. Published by Harvest House Publishers, Eugene, Oregon 97402. Used by permission.

"Tips for the Romantically Challenged" by Michael Webb condensed from *New Man* magazine. Used by permission.

"Your Best Friend" by Martha Bolton from *I Love You...Still.* Copyright © 2000 Fleming H. Revell, a division of Baker Book House Company. Used by permission.

"How to Be Happy in Marriage" by Martin F. Tupper. Public domain.

"13 Rules for Fighting Fair" by Carol Clifton, Ph.D., Clackamas, Oregon. Used by permission of the author.

"20 Creative, Romantic Ideas That Cost under $20" by Gary Smalley with John Trent from *Love Is a Decision.* Copyright © 1989, Word Publishing, Nashville, Tennessee. All rights reserved.

"The 20 Most Romantic Gifts" by Deborah Westendorf, President, The Hen's Tooth, Inc. Redmond, Oregon. Used by permission of the author.

"True Love Is..." by Dr. Gary and Barbara Rosberg condensed from *The 5 Love Needs of Men and Women* by Dr. Gary and Barbara Rosberg © 2000. Used by permission of Tyndale House Publishers. All rights reserved.

"Four Promises of Forgiveness" by Ken Sande from *The Peacemaker.* Copyright © 1991. Baker Book House Company. Used by permission.

"Six Steps Toward Reconciliation" by Dr. Gary Chapman from *Hope for the Separated* excerpted from *HomeLife* magazine. Used by permission.

"21 Things Every Couple Should Know" by Doug Fields taken from *365 Things Every Couple Should Know*. Copyright © 2000 by Doug Fields. Published by Harvest House Publishers, Eugene, Oregon 97402. Used by permission.

"How to Make Your Marriage Healthy" Jeff Herring from the *Oregonian* newspaper. Reprinted with permission of Knight Ridder/Tribune Information Services.

"His Needs, Her Needs" by Willard Harley from *His Needs, Her Needs: Basic Needs in Marriage*. Copyright © 1986 Fleming H. Revell, a division of Baker Book House Company. Used by permission.

"20 Most Romantic Literary Works" by David Kopp and Heather Harpham Kopp authors of *Love Stories God Told*. Used by permission of the authors.

"20 Most Romantic Songs" by Kyle Liedtke, Bend, Oregon. Used by permission of the author. Kyle Liedtke is a musician with two instrumental CDs to his credit and is currently the Music Director for KNLR-FM in Bend, OR.

"Ten Greatest Romance Movies" by Dan McAuley, Vancouver, Washington. Used by permission of the author.

"How to Love Him Unconditionally" by Gary Rosberg condensed from *The 5 Love Needs of Men and Women* by Dr. Gary and Barbara Rosberg © 2000. Used by permission of Tyndale House Publishers. All rights reserved.

"How to Love Her Unconditionally" by Barbara Rosberg condensed from *The 5 Love Needs of Men and Women* by Dr. Gary and Barbara Rosberg © 2000. Used by permission of Tyndale House Publishers. All rights reserved.

"Daily Tips for Your Marriage" by Glenda Hotton, M.A., C.D.C., M.F.T. Counselor for Women's Issues of Trauma/Crisis Abuse; Substance Abuse in private practice in Santa Clarita, CA. Used by permission of the author.

"When the Situation Is Difficult, Ask..." by Duane Story and Sanford Kulkin from *Body and Soul*. Copyright © 1998, Multnomah Publishers, Inc., Sisters, Oregon. Used by permission.

"Suggestions on How to Serve Your Spouse" by Gary Chapman taken from *Decision* magazine. Used by permission of the author, who has written eleven books including *The Five Love Languages* and *Hope for the Separated: Wounded Marriages Can Be Healed*.

"20 Marriage Memories" by Angela Dean Lund, Bend, Oregon. Used by permission of the author.

"Talk About These Things" by David and Claudia Arp from *Marriage Partnership* magazine, adapted from *10 Great Dates* (Zondervan, 1997) and

Love Life for Parents (Zondervan). David and Claudia Arp, founders of Marriage Alive, are educators, national speakers and seminar leaders, and authors of numerous books including *10 Great Dates* and *The Second Half of Marriage* (both Zondervan). Web site: www.marriagealive.com. E-mail: TheArps@marriagealive.com.

"Springboards to Deeper Conversation" by Carole Mayhall condensed from *Lord, Teach Me Wisdom*. Used by permission of the author.

"How to Be an Affectionate Husband" by Willard Harley from *His Needs, Her Needs: Basic Needs in Marriage*. Copyright © 1986 Fleming H. Revell, a division of Baker Book House Company. Used by permission.

"How to Find the Perfect Gift" by Tami Stephens, Clackamas, Oregon. Used by permission of the author.

"Faith Affirmations for a Husband" selected from *The Holy Bible*.

"Faith Affirmations for a Wife" selected from *The Holy Bible*.